ON A MISSION

Secret
Service
Agent

ON A MISSION

Bomb Squad Technician

Border Security

Dogs on Patrol

FBI Agent

Fighter Pilot

Firefighter

Paramedic

Search and Rescue Team

Secret Service Agent

Special Forces

SWAT Team

Undercover Police Officer

ON A MISSION

Secret Service Agent

By Tim Newcomb

Mason Crest
450 Parkway Drive, Suite D
Broomall, PA 19008
www.masoncrest.com

Printed and bound in the United States of America.

Series ISBN: 978-1-4222-3391-7
Hardback ISBN: 978-1-4222-3400-6
EBook ISBN: 978-1-4222-8509-1

First printing
1 3 5 7 9 8 6 4 2

Produced by Shoreline Publishing Group LLC
Santa Barbara, California
Editorial Director: James Buckley Jr.
Designer: Bill Madrid
Production: Sandy Gordon
www.shorelinepublishing.com
Cover photo: Newscom/Hill Street Images/Blend LLC

Library of Congress Cataloging-in-Publication Data
Newcomb, Tim, 1978-
        Secret service agent / by Tim Newcomb.
                pages cm. -- (On a mission!)
        Includes index.
ISBN 978-1-4222-3400-6 (hardback) -- ISBN 978-1-4222-3391-7 (series) -- ISBN 978-1-4222-8509-1 (ebook) 1.
United States. Secret Service--Juvenile literature. 2. Secret service--United States--Juvenile literature. I. Title.
        HV8144.S43N49 2016   363.28'302373--dc23

                                                                                    2015004837

Contents

Emergency! 6

Mission Prep 12

Training Mind and Body 20

Tools and Technology 30

Mission Accomplished! 40

Find Out More... 46

Series Glossary 47

Index/About the Author... 48

Key Icons to Look For

Words to Understand: These words with their easy-to-understand definitions will increase the reader's understanding of the text, while building vocabulary skills.

Sidebars: This boxed material within the main text allows readers to build knowledge, gain insights, explore possibilities, and broaden their perspectives by weaving together additional information to provide realistic and holistic perspectives.

Research Projects: Readers are pointed toward areas of further inquiry connected to each chapter. Suggestions are provided for projects that encourage deeper research and analysis.

Text-Dependent Questions: These questions send the reader back to the text for more careful attention to the evidence presented here.

Series Glossary of Key Terms: This back-of-the-book glossary contains terminology used throughout this series. Words found here increase the reader's ability to read and comprehend higher-level books and articles in this field.

Emergency!

President Obama has everyone's attention, but the watchful eyes of the Secret Service (glasses, rear) are monitoring the crowd for danger.

At first glance, Pennsylvania didn't seem much like a scary place for President Barack Obama to visit. It was just a few miles from his home in Washington, D.C., and home to millions of happy Americans.

The president was set to give several speeches in the state in 2013, including one at Lackawanna College, about 10 miles (16 km) from the town of Clarks Summit. Lackawanna College certainly didn't seem like a dangerous destination.

However, the only thing standing in the way of an attack on President Obama, even at Lackawanna College in Pennsylvania, is the U.S. Secret Service. It is this same agency that protects the president whether he is at home in the White House, traveling the world, or visiting Lackawanna College.

People have attacked presidents for years and years. From physical violence to gunshots, attacks come at a high price. For all the assassination attempts, there are thousands of threats that never move past the writing or talking stage. These threats have occurred since George Washington took office in 1789 and keep coming right up to today. Sometimes those threats turn deadly.

Words to Understand

apprehend arrest, take into police custody

Four U.S. Presidents have been killed by assassination, the most recent in 1963 with the death of President John F. Kennedy. Those four assassinations weren't the only attempts, and they certainly weren't the only threats.

Sometimes, attacks come out of nowhere, such as when Secret Service Agent Jerry Parr acted quickly to save President Ronald Reagan in 1981.

As President Reagan was leaving the Washington Hilton Hotel, a man later identified as John Hinckley fired a gun at him. The president was shot, and Parr leapt to action. He immediately grabbed the president and pushed him into a waiting presidential limousine. At the same time, fellow agent Timothy J. McCarthy turned toward the gunman and took a bullet in the stomach. That bullet was meant for the president. While chaos occurred outside the car, with a Secret Service agent shot and others scrambling to **apprehend** the shooter, Parr stayed with the president.

As the limo sped away, Parr ran his hands over the president looking for a wound. He soon found Reagan was coughing up blood. He had been shot in the chest. Parr instructed the driver to reach a hospital immediately. Once in George Washington Hospital, Parr's job was only starting. He and other agents had to secure the area around the hospital, making sure the building remained safe for the president.

During this dramatic turn of events, two agents, Parr and McCarthy, went above and beyond to protect the president. They didn't have time to think, instead relying on their training to

In 1981, John Hinckley (center) attempted to kill President Reagan. Secret Service agents leaped into the path of the gunfire to save the president.

react. In other situations, however, would-be killers give a warning, whether they mean to or not. From the days of assassination attempts that killed Abraham Lincoln in 1865, James Garfield in 1881, William McKinley in 1901, and John F. Kennedy in 1963 to now, there have always been attacks that require the Secret Service to step in. The threats against the president are still real, and they can still come from anywhere.

Now, though, it can be tough to figure out what people really mean when they write online. Threats against the president used to be just badly written letters. Today, the *Washington Post* reports that more than 60 percent of all threats against the president are made online. Emails, social media, and other formats give would-be attackers a way to make more threats. The Secret Service has even started looking at computer software that can help to scan social media posts and emails to detect whether someone is joking or not.

Whether received online or through the mail, all threats are taken seriously by the Secret Service.

While the threats may not all be real or the people behind them may not always follow up, the Service doesn't want to miss the one that matters most.

That included one that came from a man near Lackawanna College.

In August 2013, someone posted this message on the White House Web site: "President Obama the Anti-Christ, as a result of breaking the Constitution you will stand down or be shot dead." The writer followed that up by saying he was sending out a call to action. Immediately, the Secret Service took notice. It didn't want another assassination attempt on its hands.

Could the Secret Service find where this threat came from? Could it find who this person was? Could it find this person in time? Finally, what did Lackawanna College have to do with it?

Later, in this book's final chapter, "Mission Accomplished," find out how the Secret Service dealt with this threat. First, read the story of how this brave unit protects American leaders and currency.

Chapter 1

The U.S. Secret Service is best known for the protectors who travel with the president, but it also has a very visible uniformed presence at the White House.

Mission Prep

The most visible job for the agents of the U.S. Secret Service is protecting the president. That protection happens in a variety of ways. Many agents wear uniforms, working at the White House—the home of the president in Washington, D.C.—to guard the building and anyone in it. Those agents work as part of the "uniformed division." The agents who work right alongside the president and other top government officials, are the "protection division." They keep a close watch on the people around the president or whomever they are protecting.

Secret Service agents also work on what is called threat **assessment** and advance teams. These agents spend time figuring out possible dangers to the president before he travels. Every possible threat against the safety of the president requires an entire team of agents to investigate. Plus, before the president travels—and he travels often—an advance team plans the safest routes and best ways to allow the president to move around a city or foreign country.

Words to Understand

assassination the act of killing an elected or appointed government official, usually a nation's leader

assessment the act of gathering information and making a decision about a particular topic

Protecting the President

Helping guard the president can be a dangerous job. In fact, a few Secret Service agents have been wounded or killed while guarding the president or other people. In 1950, while protecting President Harry Truman, Officer Leslie Coffelt lost his life during an assassination attempt. In 1981, when someone tried to kill President Ronald Reagan, Special Agent Tim McCarthy stepped in to protect him, and was shot. McCarthy was able to recover from his injury. Special Agent Nick Zarvos was also shot protecting a U.S. governor who was trying to become president. Zarvos helped save the life of the governor, and both men recovered from the attack.

Multiple Missions

The U.S. Secret Service was established by President Abraham Lincoln on April 14, 1865. Lincoln signed the legislation only hours before he was shot by John Wilkes Booth at Ford's Theatre that night.

The new agency, however, was actually formed as part of the Department of the Treasury to combat counterfeiting, the act of making fake money. Such crimes can cost the government millions, as well as disrupt or even ruin private businesses. In 1865, nearly one-third of all the money used in the United States was counterfeit. It wasn't until 1901, when President William McKinley was shot and killed, that the Secret Service also started to protect the president.

Today, the Secret Service still has those main responsibilities: protect the president and other important government workers; and investigate crimes, especially relating to money. Agents today also work to stop forms of cybercrime, the type that happens with a

Stopping people who are making fake money—counterfeiters—is another big job for the Secret Service.

The most secure aircraft in the world is staffed by Secret Service agents whenever the president travels.

computer. Agents must work to keep people from using computers to create false identities, stop the theft of U.S. stocks and bonds (a different form of money), help protect banks, and work to stop any other crime that can happen with the use of a computer.

The life of people working for the Secret Service can mean a lot of different things. They can be someone running alongside the president's limousine or flying in the president's airplane—Air Force One—looking for danger and being willing to step in and fight anyone seeking to harm the president. They can also be an agent working in an office trying to locate the people responsible for creating and selling fake money.

To join the agency, a person needs a college degree. From there, though, plenty of different types of personalities can find a perfect fit in the Secret Service. Many agents and support personnel work in the department's main headquarters in Washington, D.C. (Not surprisingly, the headquarters is in a large downtown building without any signs to help keep the Secret Service a little more secret.) Agents also work in 150 field offices around the world. Whether working in London, England; Portland, Maine; Bogota, Colombia; or Portland, Ore., the agents go where they are needed to stop lawbreakers.

Just in case: When protestors threaten to get too close to the White House, Secret Service personnel are on the job.

The jobs within the U.S. Secret Service are quite varied. The agency includes 3,200 special agents, 1,300 uniformed officers, and more than 2,000 other technical, professional, and administrative support personnel. It takes a lot of different types of personalities and interests to ensure that the agency runs well. The jobs can, and do, take place in every state in the United States, as well as in places around the world. Still, the jobs all have one requirement in common: a desire to work hard in order to best understand how to stop criminals from hurting both the president and the citizens of the United States.

Text-Dependent Questions

1. What are the roles of the two main branches of the Secret Service?
2. Describe some of the different types of jobs within the U.S. Secret Service agency.
3. Where is the U.S. Secret Service headquarters located? Are there offices in other countries outside of the United States?

Research Project

Find out why counterfeiting was such a problem in the 1800s and what did the government do to try and stop it.

Chapter 2

Every Secret Service agent has to maintain a high level of fitness in order to do the job well.

Training Mind and Body

It takes years of training just to prepare to become a U.S. Secret Service Agent. Once hired onto the team, though, the learning doesn't stop.

All agents must be successful in school, working hard to get into college and earn a degree. After applying to the Service and being selected, new agents get additional training at the Federal Law Enforcement Training Center in Glynco, Georgia. They undergo a 12-week Criminal Investigator Training Program, designed to help them learn about the law, how to investigate cases, and the best way to do their job.

Training Academy

Once agents pass the initial training in Georgia, they attend a longer Special Agent Training Course. This course gives the new agents all the

Words to Understand

detail in the Secret Service, a small group of agents assigned to a particular task or protection assignment

marksmanship a measurement of the skill of a person at using firearms

motorcade a long procession of vehicles traveling together

Real or fake? These bills are all real and demonstrate anti-counterfeiting designs created with help from the Secret Service.

information they need about the jobs in the Secret Service, whether investigative or protective. At the James J. Rowley Training Center near Washington, D.C., agents have 500 acres (200 hectares) of land, six miles (10 km) of roads, and 31 buildings to give them a wide variety of opportunities to develop their protection skills. They also receive advanced training in how to spot and stop counterfeiting and other electronic crimes.

Agents also learn about **marksmanship**, with lots of time spent on the gun range. There are plenty of special extras for Secret Service agents at the training center, including fake villages with buildings to train in, and even a partial mock-up of the Air Force One airplane used by the president.

Physical fitness is key to life in the Service. Agents must always be in top-notch physical

They don't want to shoot, but when they do, Secret Service agents need to be experts with firearms.

Always on the job, Secret Service agents watch over the president even in the safety of the White House's Oval Office.

shape. From basic physical fitness like you might expect in a P.E. class all the way to physical protection training such as self-defense, and even underwater survival skills, the physical nature of the job starts with the proper training. Agents learn about emergency medicine they can use in the field. Agents also train on the many types of communications gear they will use in the field.

After becoming a full agent, the training never stops. Agents take refresher courses on medicine, self-defense, and guns, along with new techniques in fighting counterfeiting or recognizing threats to the people they protect. Every extra learning experience makes sure agents have the right tools to do the job.

Crisis Training

Agents assigned to protective details take part in crisis-training situations. These real-looking tests are designed to help agents make quick decisions about how they should respond, and then let them know if they made the right decisions.

Much of the Secret Service training work focuses on both the mind and the body, often at the same time. Physical fitness and marksmanship are a key part of the job, but being able to be effective in a real-life situation also requires agents to use their minds to make smart, fast decisions. The crisis training puts agents into situations they might face in the field, such as a gunman going for the president or a bomber threatening a **motorcade**. The more the future agents can practice what they might face in real life, the better chance they and the people they protect have to survive.

To help keep the agents sharp, ongoing training includes all kinds of courses designed to help them better work with each other and better understand the types of crimes occurring in the real world. Some of this work includes classroom-type learning so that agents know the rules, laws, and tools that will help them do their job properly.

One of the most important parts of Secret Service training—as well as a key reason for their success—is teamwork. In their training, agents learn how to work and respond as a team, knowing that each member will do his or her part.

Once they become agents, they are still learning. New experiences can come with each new assignment. For example, Secret Service agents who have worked with two recent presidents had to re-learn something they probably learned as kids: how to ride a bicycle. Presidents George W. Bush and Barack Obama both ride bicycles "relatively quickly," says the Secret Service. This created a bit of a challenge for Secret Service agents required to stay with the presidents to protect them. The agents assigned to the presidential **detail** had to be expert riders to deal with any threat that arose while on two wheels. If agents are spending all their time trying to keep up on a

bicycle, they won't be able to focus on watching the area around them for any potential threats or dangers.

In the same way, keeping their mind sharp helps agents know when to pick up clues or spot potential danger out from among the crowd. Training to be a U.S. Special Agent isn't a one-time deal. Agents must learn as much as possible in the early days of their training, but they also must always be

Can you spot the agents? They are always near the president and, in this case, First Lady Michelle Obama. Look for the lapel pins to find agents.

willing to learn new tools along the way—even if that means riding a bicycle a little faster.

Taking a Bullet If Needed

With intensive physical training and great team-work, Secret Service agents are ready for any task. When investigating a counterfeiting crime, they use computers, interviews, and other tools. When they locate a suspect, they work with local police to make the arrest.

When they are working in the protection division, however, there is another layer of train-ing. The agents need to be ready literally to give their lives to do their work. This is an enormous responsibility and calls for a person of real mental strength. Agents assigned to the president have normally worked their way up to this top detail by working with Cabinet secretaries or the vice-president. Other agents learned their skills helping protect the families of top officials.

When they make the presidential detail, they are at the center of the action all the time, working in the White House and traveling with the president. They can be seen in photos and on TV near him at all times. Look for the steely-eyed men and women wearing earpieces. They're the ones who are not looking at the president, but at everything around him.

They don't want to get shot, but they are willing to sacrifice their bodies and their lives to do their job. Few people in any job face such a possible outcome every day they go to work—but that's life in the Secret Service.

Text-Dependent Questions

1. What kind of medical training do agents take?
2. Someone with good marksmanship scores is good at what skill?
3. What did agents have to learn to keep up with Presidents George W. Bush and Barack Obama?

Research Project

Find out how other nations protect their leaders. Do they have agencies like the Secret Service? Does the military do that job in some places? How are other countries different or similar to ours in this respect?

Chapter 3

Quick and dependable communication is vital to any Secret Service operation. In-ear receivers and lapel or wrist microphones make that possible.

Tools and Technology

The U.S. Secret Service uses a wide variety of gear and technology to get multiple jobs done.

Communications

The best-known piece of Secret Service gear is the earpiece that every agent wears. You can often see the wire connected to it running down an agent's neck and into his or her clothing. Today's tiny earpieces started decades ago as a way to connect Secret Service personnel via radio. Today's earpieces connect to hidden microphones worn on a Secret Service agent's body—often under the shirtsleeve, which is why you see agents hold their hand near their mouth. These systems can also be **encrypted**, which means that only a person with the right code can hear what is being said. This ensures that all communication between the Secret Service agents remains private and secret.

Words to Understand

ballistic having to do with high velocity

dignitary a person of high government rank or community status

encrypted put into code or blocked from being shared

forensics the science of crime investigation

magnification the process of using lenses and devices to make far-away objects appear much closer

31

The shades look good, but they are worn for a reason. By hiding their eyes, agents can watch people without giving their target away.

Dressed to Protect

In photos and on TV, we often see Secret Service agents wearing dark sunglasses and suits. Those sunglasses are not just for looking good. They help agents do their job by keeping the sun away from their eyes, and also shielding someone else from figuring out exactly where they are looking.

As for the suits, those who are protecting the president or some other **dignitary** wear whatever must be worn to blend in. Often they will wear business suits, since most of the meetings or travel are for business. Other times they have dressed up as a professional sport referee, worn a military uniform, or even donned a jogging suit while running with their detail.

Eyes in the Sky

Not everyone in the protection division walks alongside the president. The Secret Service Countersniper Unit uses specially built weapons and equipment designed just for the Service. This team takes positions from the roof of the White House aimed at buildings in a city where the president visits. They provide long-range protection of the president with their unique weapons. High-**magnification** scopes on their rifles can help them track possible threats. The agents using those rifles are top marksmen, able to hit a target from hundreds of yards away.

Air Force One

Any aircraft carrying the president is called Air Force One, but the plane he most commonly uses is a Boeing 747-200B. This is not like any other airplane you've ever flown in. Air Force One is larger than an average house in the United States and has all kinds of specialized equipment. Its communications gear lets the president conduct emergency business without anyone being able to see or hear. An onboard operating room is staffed by doctors whenever the president flies. The airplane is surrounded by high-tech armor. The Secret Service lives up to its name as well; it says there are other protective measures on the president's plane that are kept…secret.

Body Armor and More

Secret Service vehicles that accompany the president carry submachine guns, extra pistols, and ammunition. They carry flashlights that are more powerful than a car's headlights. Agents have night-vision goggles that allow them to see in the dark. Agents near the president can also wear additional protection, such as bulletproof vests. These vests are made of Kevlar, a material five times stronger than steel, and, though not completely bulletproof, can protect against many types of assault.

Sometimes protecting the body means protecting the place you are in. The Secret Service is always researching the best and latest in **ballistic** glass, which is a type of glass that will not shatter or break when hit with a bullet or a bomb. This glass can be used in buildings, airplanes, and the president's limousine.

Not only does the president's car have glass that can't be broken, but everything about the car is different than what a typical family drives around town. The fuel tank is armor-plated and covered in foam so that even if a bullet does hit it, the tank won't explode and injure anyone. The entire car has a system in it to put out fires instantly. In the trunk are weapons, oxygen supplies, emergency medical equipment, and even extra blood in case

Designed to look similar to a regular passenger car, the presidential vehicles are packed with security and protective gear.

the president needs a blood infusion to keep him alive. Remember that emergency medical training the agents took?

The armor-plated car is so thick and heavy that it can seal off the outside from getting in, even if toxic air is all around the car. The tires have Kevlar in them so they can't go flat. Inside the car, the president has all the latest in radio and video equipment so he can talk to the outside world.

Detecting Tech

For work on investigations, the Secret Service uses some pretty high-tech tools. The agency's Instrument Analysis Services Section includes the International Ink Library, the world's largest such collection. In this advanced **forensics** laboratory, the Secret Service can examine all types of evidence—from counterfeit money to computers—to catch criminals and prove who did the crimes.

The ink library serves as just one of those tools. With more than 10,000 samples of inks, agents can determine the type and brand of ink used and when that ink likely was created. Within the lab is also the largest database of paper types in the world. Using forensic science, agents can determine what type of paper was used and even what type of tree the paper came from, which is useful in finding a counterfeit moneymaker. With that kind of information, agents can then figure out where the paper was made and maybe even where it was sold. Because the act of making counterfeit money often uses more than just paper and ink, the Secret Service also has a collection of images, plastics, and other materials that help them find everything they need to know to investigate a counterfeit crime.

In addition, using scientific methods, the scientists and researchers within this specialized Secret Service unit can help agents determine facts about weapons used in crimes.

Ink Fingerprints

The Secret Service's International Ink Library can take a "fingerprint" of any ink from any paper on any letter. A relatively new Digital Ink Library makes finding the information Secret Service agents need a lot easier to find. In past decades, agents would have to flip through pages and pages of books to find a match. Now, the database lets agents type in a search to quickly identify matches in ink. Using solvents to separate ink into bands of color, Secret Service agents can determine an ink's unique fingerprint. With all that information loaded into a database, investigators spend less time trying to find the correct ink and more time trying to find the criminal.

Secret Service agents act as long-range spotters when the president is out in public. Some spotters work in tandem with snipers to be able to eliminate threats from a distance.

On the Watch

Finding the ink and paper—or keeping tabs on someone who has threatened the president—sometimes requires a lot of surveillance. That means following and watching someone to find out what that person is doing. To successfully follow a criminal, agents need the latest in computer abilities, recording devices, voice-identification equipment, and much more.

The Secret Service uses the latest in surveillance gear, including remote microphones, listening "bugs," and even visual coverage of a suspect, to keep an eye on potential threats.

Sometimes a person communicates a threat to the president, but does so anonymously. With the help of the Forensic Services Division, which can look at everything from a person's voice to the way he or she writes letters, agents can often track that person down and make an arrest.

Being physically and mentally ready is key for all Secret Service agents, but having the right tools and technology means they are always ready to do the job.

Text-Dependent Questions

1. What specialized group in the Secret Service do you think has the most interesting job?
2. Name two key pieces of equipment used by those protecting people. Now name two used by those investigating crimes.
3. What tool or technology do you think is the most unique to the Secret Service?

Research Project

Find an example of an old Secret Service tool and show how it looks in modern days.

Chapter 4

Before the president gives a speech anywhere, the Secret Service carefully checks out the location and the people who will attend.

Mission Accomplished!

The Secret Service is always on the watch for threats to the president. In 2013, the agency got a nasty one via the White House Web site. It set about tracking down the writer, who had actually signed his name, "Nick Savino," to the post, but that could have meant anything. It could have been an alias. Or, as it turned out, it could have been the real name of the person writing the threat.

The Secret Service went into full cybertracking mode. Using computer technology available to the Secret Service, it was able to track the post to the location of the computer on which the post was made. The investigation led their agents to Clarks Summit, Pennsylvania., just 10 miles (16 km) from Lackawanna College, where President Obama had an upcoming date to speak.

Words to Understand
alias a fake name that someone (such as a criminal) might use

If a threat is discovered in time, the Secret Service has the personnel to make an arrest before something bad can happen.

As part of investigating every threat against the president and making sure areas he travels to remain safe, the Secret Service needed to do more with their information on Savino.

They found out everything they needed to know about this man, an engineer who lived in the area for less than a year. Then they acted.

With the help of the Clarks Summit Police and the Lackawanna County SWAT team working on behalf of the Secret Service, the law enforcement personnel went into Savino's apartment and vehicle. They found three guns and 11,000 rounds of ammunition. Police arrested Savino and ended any potential threat to the president, only a day before he was scheduled to be in town.

Thanks to the Secret Service, Savino never got the chance to act on his threat. Agents found him with their cybersecurity and cybertracking methods, and then everyone involved bravely stepped in to make the arrest. If they hadn't acted so quickly the day before the president was to speak at the nearby college, we may have heard of Lackawanna College for a horrible reason.

There are plenty of other cases of the Secret Service stepping in to save a president. In 1975, when a woman tried to shoot President Gerald Ford, a Secret Service agent tackled her before she could fire her gun. In the 1960s, a would-be assassin of President Lyndon B. Johnson tipped off the FBI to his plan, and the Secret Service stepped in to help arrest him before he could board a train to Washington, D.C.

Secret Service in the News

In 2014, the Secret Service was in the news, but not in a good way. Twice that year, people leaped the fence at the White House and tried to reach the building. One man even made it in through an open door. The uniformed agents of the Secret Service were criticized for letting the people get so close to the White House. As a result, new procedures were put in place to make the president's house even more secure. The Secret Service was embarrassed, but it responded by continuing to improve.

In the 1970s, a wealthy banker requested an appointment with President Richard Nixon. After running a background check on the man, Andrew B. Topping, the Secret Service decided to interview him. Through its investigation, it found Topping had started asking others about the possibility of hiring someone to kill the president. The Secret Service wanted to catch him in the act and sent an agent undercover to pose as an assassin. After a negotiation at the boat basin in New York's Central Park, Topping agreed to pay the undercover agent to kill the president. Topping was arrested on the spot.

In every case, from years ago to threats against the current president, Secret Service training and expertise ensures the safety of the president and many other important people in the government. The Secret Service also makes sure our vital money supply is safe.

What about that trip to Lackawanna? In 2013, President Obama's trip to Pennsylvania turned out to be as routine as ever. He was able to keep his appointments. Because of the Secret Service, most of us had never heard of Lackawanna College until reading this book.

The Secret Service is always on the watch for trouble, ready to give their lives to protect the president.

Find Out More

Books

Emmett, Dan. *Within Arm's Length: The Extraordinary Life and Career of a Special Agent in the United States Secret Service.* iUniverse, 2012.

Holden, Henry. *To Be a U.S. Secret Service Agent.* Minneapolis: Zenith Press, 2006.

Parr, Jerry and Parr, Carolyn. *In the Secret Service: The True Story of the Man Who Saved President Reagan's Life.* Carol Stream, Ill.: Tyndale House Publishers, Inc., 2013.

Web Sites

United States Secret Service
www.secretservice.gov

Inside the Secret Service (from *The Atlantic* magazine)
www.theatlantic.com/magazine/archive/2011/03/inside-the-secret-service/308390/

The Making of an Agent (from *The Washington Post* magazine)
www.washingtonpost.com/wp-dyn/content/article/2009/07/17/AR

Series Glossary of Key Terms

apprehending capturing and arresting someone who has committed a crime

assassinate kill somebody, especially a political figure

assessment the act of gathering information and making a decision about a particular topic

contraband material that is illegal to possess

cryptography another word for writing in code

deployed put to use, usually in a military or law-enforcement operation

dispatcher a person who announces emergencies over police radio and helps organize the efforts of first responders

elite among the very best; part of a select group of successful experts

evacuated moved to a safe location, away from danger

federal related to the government of the United States, as opposed to the government of an individual state or city

forensic having to do with crime scene evidence

instinctive based on natural impulse and done without instruction

interrogate to question a person as part of an official investigation

Kevlar an extra-tough fabric used in bulletproof vests

search-and-rescue the work of finding survivors after a disaster occurs, or the team that does this work

stabilize make steady or secure; also, in medicine, make a person safe to transport

surveillance the act of watching another person or a place, usually from a hidden location

trauma any physical injury to the body, usually involving bleeding

visa travel permit issued by a government to a citizen for a specific trip

warrant official document that allows the police to do something, such as arrest a person

Index

Air Force One 17, 23, 34

body armor 34

Booth, John Wilkes 14

Bush, President George W. 26

communications gear 31, 32

counterfeiting 14, 15, 15, 22, 36, 37

Department of the Treasury 14

Digital Ink Library 37

Federal Law Enforcement Training Center 21

Ford, President Gerald 43

Hinckley, John 8, 9

Instrument Analysis Services Section 36

James J. Rowley Training Center 22

Kennedy, President John 8, 10

Lackawanna College 7, 11, 41, 45

limousine, presidential 34

Lincoln, President Abraham 10, 14

McCarthy, Timothy J. 8, 9, 14

McKinley, President William 10, 14

Nixon, President Richard 44

Obama, President Barack 7, 11, 26, 27, 41, 45

Parr, Jerry 8, 9

Reagan, President Ronald 8, 9

Secret Service Countersniper Unit 33

surveillance gear 38, 39

SWAT team 42

Washington, D.C. 7, 13, 17, 22, 43

White House 7, 11, 13, 24, 29

Zarvos, Nick 14

Photo Credits

About the Author

Tim Newcomb is a freelance journalist based in the Pacific Northwest. He writes for *Sports Illustrated* and *Popular Mechanics* about sports design and engineering. His work has also appeared in *Time*, *Wired*, *Fast Company*, *Dwell*, *Stadia*, and a variety of publications around the world.

Dedicated to my daughters, Adia, Kalanie, and Rilanna, and the pursuit of their own missions!–T.N.